10 Essential Lessons

1 Respect

RESPECT OTHERS, NO MATTER WHAT THEIR BACKGROUND OR BELIEFS ARE.

2 Kindness

BE KIND AND COMPASSIONATE TO OTHERS.

3 Responsibility

BE RESPONSIBLE FOR YOUR ACTIONS AND TAKE OWNERSHIP OF YOUR MISTAKES.

4 Honesty

ALWAYS TELL THE TRUTH, EVEN IF IT'S DIFFICULT.

5 Perseverance

NEVER GIVE UP AND KEEP TRYING, EVEN WHEN THINGS GET TOUGH.

6 Creativity

USE YOUR IMAGINATION AND CREATIVITY TO SOLVE PROBLEMS AND CREATE NEW THINGS.

7 Empathy

PUT YOURSELF IN OTHER PEOPLE'S SHOES TO UNDERSTAND HOW THEY MIGHT BE FEELING.

8 Gratitude

BE GRATEFUL FOR WHAT YOU HAVE AND APPRECIATE THE PEOPLE IN YOUR LIFE.

9 Teamwork

WORK TOGETHER WITH OTHERS TO ACHIEVE COMMON GOALS.

10 Confidence

BELIEVE IN YOURSELF AND YOUR ABILITIES, AND DO NOT BE AFRAID TO TAKE RISKS OR TRY NEW THINGS.

Respect

This story will be inspiring because it teaches the importance of treating everyone with kindness and respect, regardless of their differences. It shows that when you learn about each other's habits and customs, you can create a more inclusive and welcoming community. When you respect and value each other, you can live in a world where diversity is celebrated, and everyone feels included.

The Magic of Respect: Embracing Differences

In a vast forest, there were many animals of different species living together in harmony. They respected each other and lived peacefully. One day, a new animal arrived in the forest, but it was different from any other animal the forest dwellers had ever seen. The new animal had unique features and strange habits, which made the other animals feel unsure about how to react.

The wise old owl noticed that the new animal was feeling isolated and alone, so he called a meeting of all the animals in the forest. During the meeting, the owl reminded everyone of the importance of respect and inclusion. He explained that every animal deserves to be treated with kindness and respect, regardless of their differences. He encouraged the animals to learn about the new animal's habits and customs and to treat them with kindness and respect.

The animals took the owl's words to heart and soon welcomed the new animal with open arms. They learned about the new animal's unique features and habits and incorporated them into their own lives. The new animal felt valued and included, and the forest became an even more beautiful place where diversity was celebrated.

Kindness

This story is heartwarming because it teaches you the value of being kind to others. It shows that even a small act of kindness, like helping someone in need, can make a big difference in their life. When you show kindness to others, you can create a world that is full of love and happiness. It reminds you that you should always be kind to everyone you meet.

The Power of Kindness: Make the World a better place

There was a little girl named Alice. She was a very kind and gentle girl who always had a smile on her face. One day, while walking in the park, she saw an old man sitting on a bench with a sad look on his face. Alice walked up to him and asked, "Are you okay, sir? Is there anything I can do to help you?" The old man looked at her and smiled. "Thank you for asking, little one. I'm just feeling a bit lonely today."

Alice didn't hesitate for a second. She sat down next to the old man and started talking to him. She told him about her day and her favorite things to do. The old man listened to her and smiled. He started to feel better. After a while, Alice had to go home. She said goodbye to the old man and gave him a big hug. The old man felt so grateful for Alice's kindness and decided to come to the park every day to see her.

From that day on, Alice and the old man became good friends. They would meet in the park every day and talk about their lives. Alice learned a lot from the old man, and the old man enjoyed spending time with her. Alice's kindness made a big difference in the old man's life. He no longer felt lonely, and he looked forward to seeing Alice every day. Alice had also learned an important lesson. She realized that a small act of kindness can make someone's day and even change their life. And so, Alice continued to spread kindness wherever she went, and she inspired others to do the same.

Responsibility

This story teaches the importance of being responsible for their belongings. It shows that when we are responsible, you can avoid losing things or causing problems. It also teaches that being responsible can have positive effects on our lives and those around us and that it is a valuable trait to have.

The Power of Responsibility: Taking Care of What Matters

There was a girl named Alice who loved taking care of her things. She had a lot of belongings, but she always put them back where they belonged after using them. Her parents were proud of her for being so responsible, and they often praised her for it.

One day, Alice's favorite necklace went missing. She looked for it everywhere, but it was nowhere to be found. Her parents asked her if she had put it away properly, and Alice had to admit that she had not. She felt sad and disappointed that her carelessness had caused her to lose her favorite necklace.

Alice learned her lesson and promised to be even more responsible in the future. She started putting her things away after using them and even helped her parents with other chores around the house. One day, while cleaning her room, she found her missing necklace. She was overjoyed and realized that being responsible was not only important, but it also had its rewards.

Honesty

This comical story teaches the importance of honesty. It shows that lying can have funny and unexpected consequences, but that it is always better to tell the truth. You will learn that honesty is a valuable trait to have and that it can make them feel good about themselves.

The Nose That Knew: The Power of Honesty

There was a girl named Alice who loved eating candy. One day, her mom left a bag of candy on the table and Alice couldn't resist the temptation. She sneaked into the kitchen and ate a piece of candy.

When her mom saw the missing candy, she asked Alice if she had taken it. Alice, not wanting to get in trouble, lied and said she didn't know anything about it. Suddenly, something strange started happening. Alice's nose began to grow longer and longer, just like Pinocchio's!

Alice was surprised and didn't know what was happening. Her mom saw her nose and knew that she was lying. She told her that lying was not okay and that honesty is always the best policy. Alice felt embarrassed and ashamed that she had lied, but she learned her lesson.

From that day on, Alice always told the truth, no matter what. And her nose never grew long again. She even found that telling the truth made her feel better, even if she got in trouble sometimes.

Perseverance

This story teaches the importance of perseverance. It shows that even when things get tough, it is important to keep trying and never give up. With hard work and dedication, you can achieve your goals and create beautiful things. You will learn that success often comes after many failed attempts and that the key to success is to keep going, even when it feels hard.

The Triumph of Perseverance: Never Giving Up on Your Dreams

There was a girl named Alice who loved to play basketball. She spent hours every day practicing and perfecting her skills, but one day, she became frustrated. No matter how hard she tried, she just couldn't get her shots to go into the basket.

Alice wanted to give up, but her dad encouraged her to keep trying. He reminded her that every athlete goes through times when they feel like they can't get it right and that the only way to get better was to keep practicing.

Alice took her dad's advice and kept playing basketball. Even when things got tough and she felt like giving up, she kept going. She tried new techniques and kept practicing until she finally achieved the results she wanted.

And one day, after many hours of practice, Alice scored a three-pointer. It was a beautiful shot, with every detail just right. She felt proud of herself and realized that if she had given up, she would have never achieved her goal.

Creativity

This story teaches the importance of using their imagination and creativity to solve problems and create new things. It shows that sometimes when things don't go as planned, you can use your creativity to turn a negative situation into a positive one. You will learn that by using their imagination, they can create amazing things and have fun in the process.

Unleashing the Power of Creativity: Turning Challenges into Masterpieces

There was a girl named Alice who loved to draw. She would spend hours every day creating beautiful pictures of everything she saw. One day, her little friend accidentally spilled water on one of her drawings, and it started to smudge.

Alice was upset at first, but then she had an idea. She started to use her imagination and creativity to turn the smudged drawing into something new. Before she knew it, she had created a beautiful painting out of the smudged drawing!

Alice looked at her painting and felt proud of herself. She realized that by using her imagination and creativity, she had turned a negative situation into a positive one. She even showed her little friend how to make his own painting out of a smudged drawing.

Together, they created new paintings and explored new techniques, all using their imagination and creativity.

Empathy

This story teaches the importance of putting themselves in other people's shoes and understanding how they might be feeling. It shows that sometimes, you need to think about how your actions might affect others and try to be kind and understanding. You will learn that by putting yourself in other people's shoes, you can become more empathetic and caring toward others

The Power of Empathy: Learning to Understand and Care for Others

There was a girl named Alice who loved to play with her toys. She had a favorite toy tablet that she loved to play with every day. One day, Alice's little sister came into the room and asked if she could play with the tablet.

Alice didn't want to share her favorite tablet, so she said no. Her little sister started to cry, and Alice felt bad. But she still didn't want to share her toy.

Later that day, Alice's mom asked her how she would feel if someone didn't want to share their favorite toy with her. Alice thought about it and realized that she would feel sad and left out.

Alice went back to her little sister and apologized for not sharing her tablet. She gave her the tablet to play with, and they started to play together. Alice realized that it was fun to share and play together and that it made her feel happy to see her sister having fun.

Gratitude

The story teaches the transformative effects of appreciating the blessings in their lives and finding joy in the simple moments.

The Magic of Gratitude: Finding Happiness in the Little Things

There was a little girl named Alice. She had everything she needed - a loving family, a comfortable home, and plenty of toys to play with. But despite having so much, she was sometimes unhappy and ungrateful. One day, Alice's family took her on a trip to a nearby village. As they walked through the streets, they saw children who didn't have many toys or fancy clothes. Some of them even had to work instead of going to school.

Alice was surprised to see that these children were still happy and smiling. They played games with each other and laughed together, even though they didn't have much. As they were leaving the village, Alice turned to her parents and said, "I have so much, but I cry and am ungrateful sometimes. Those kids don't have much, but they seem so content. Why is that?"

Her parents smiled and replied, "It's because they are grateful for what they have. They appreciate their families, their friends, and the little things in life. They know that happiness doesn't come from having a lot of things, but from being grateful for the things they do have." From that day on, Alice learned to be grateful for her family, her home, and all the things she had. She started to appreciate the people in her life and the things they did for her. And she realized that happiness comes from within, not from the things we have.

Teamwork

The story teaches the importance of teamwork, showing how combining strengths and supporting one another can lead to the realization of shared dreams. It encourages kids like you that working together amplifies their abilities and fosters a sense of accomplishment.

The Power of Teamwork: Building Dreams Together

There was a group of kids who wanted to build a treehouse in their backyard. They all loved spending time outdoors and thought a treehouse would be the perfect addition to their play area. The kids were excited about the project, but they quickly realized that building a treehouse wasn't easy. They needed to design a blueprint, gather materials, and figure out how to construct the treehouse safely. They knew they couldn't do it alone.

So, they decided to work together to achieve their goal. They divided the tasks among themselves based on their strengths and interests. The artistic kid drew the blueprint, the math whiz calculated the angles and measurements, and the handy kid helped gather the materials and tools they needed. Each day, they would come together and work on a different part of the treehouse. They worked hard and faced some challenges along the way, but they never gave up. They encouraged each other and reminded themselves of their common goal - to build the best treehouse ever!

Finally, after weeks of hard work, the treehouse was complete! It was a beautiful and sturdy structure, with a slide, a swing, and a lookout tower. The kids were thrilled with their creation and couldn't wait to play in it. But more than that, they were proud of themselves for working together to achieve their goal. They realized that by combining their strengths and skills, they could accomplish anything they set their minds to. And they learned that working together is always better than working alone. From that day on, the kids worked together on many other projects, always remembering the lessons they learned while building their amazing treehouse.

Confidence

This story teaches the importance of taking risks, believing in oneself, and embracing new challenges. It encourages young kids like you to overcome self-doubt, embrace their capabilities, and embrace the beauty of growth through exploration.

The Courageous Journey: Finding Confidence in the Wilderness

There was a little girl named Alice. She was someone who often doubted her abilities. She was afraid to try new things and take risks because she didn't want to fail or make mistakes. One day, Alice's class went on a field trip to a nearby nature reserve. They were going to go on a hike and explore the beautiful trails and wildlife. Alice was nervous because she had never gone on a hike before and didn't want to hold her classmates back.

As they started the hike, Alice's fear began to grow. She stumbled over rocks and roots, and her classmates seemed to be walking much faster than her. She was about to give up and turn back when she heard a rustling in the bushes. Out popped a friendly-looking fox who seemed to be leading them down a different path. Alice's classmates were hesitant, but Alice felt a surge of courage within her. She decided to follow the fox and see where it would lead them. As they walked, Alice felt herself becoming more and more confident. She pointed out interesting plants and animals along the way, and her classmates were impressed with her knowledge. They even started to ask her questions and listen to her stories.

Finally, the fox led them to a beautiful clearing with a waterfall and a stunning view. Alice felt a sense of pride and accomplishment wash over her. She had taken a risk and it had paid off. She believed in herself and her abilities, and it led her to an amazing experience. From that day on, Alice was more willing to try new things and take risks. She had learned that sometimes, the best things in life come from stepping outside of our comfort zones and believing in ourselves. And she had the friendly fox to thank for showing her the way.

Made in United States
Troutdale, OR
07/21/2024